The Fourth Estate
Journalism in North America

Yellow Journalism, Sensationalism, and Circulation Wars

Brett Griffin

Cavendish
Square

New York

Published in 2019 by Cavendish Square Publishing, LLC
243 5th Avenue, Suite 136, New York, NY 10016

Library of Congress Cataloging-in-Publication Data

Names: Griffin, Brett, author.
Title: Yellow journalism, sensationalism,
and circulation wars / Brett Griffin.
Description: First edition. | New York : Cavendish Square, 2019. |
Series: The fourth estate: journalism in North America |
Includes bibliographical references and index.
Identifiers: LCCN 2017058838 (print) | LCCN 2018008830 (ebook) | ISBN
9781502634726 (e-Book) | ISBN 9781502634719 (library bound) |
ISBN 9781502634733 (pbk.) | ISBN 9781502634740 (6 pack)
Subjects: LCSH: Sensationalism in journalism—United States—History—19th
century—Juvenile literature. | Journalism—United States—History—19th
century—Juvenile literature. | Spanish-American War, 1898—Press
coverage—Juvenile literature. | Spanish-American War,
1898—Causes—Juvenile literature.
Classification: LCC PN4784.S4 (ebook) | LCC PN4784.S4 G75 2019 (print) |
DDC 071.309/04--dc23
LC record available at https://lccn.loc.gov/2017058838

Editorial Director: David McNamara
Editor: Caitlyn Miller
Copy Editor: Nathan Heidelberger
Associate Art Director: Amy Greenan
Designer: Lindsey Auten
Production Coordinator: Karol Szymczuk
Photo Research: J8 Media

Printed in the United States of America

CONTENTS

The Fourth Estate

Journalism in North America

R0455403817

Technological innovations in the nineteenth century revolutionized the newspaper industry. This printing press from the early 1800s would not have been capable of handling the volume of papers printed on a daily basis at the end of the century.

A New Kind of Paper: Journalism in the Late Nineteenth Century

"From a news point of view, there are two classes of paper in New York—the *Journal* and all the others." This bold claim was printed in the August 1, 1897, issue of the *New York Journal*. It was a statement that indicated the state of the newspaper industry in New York City in the closing years of the nineteenth century. A new style of journalism had emerged over the preceding decades, one that recognized the problems with contemporary American society and actively spoke out against them. The most famous architects of this new journalism were William Randolph Hearst, owner and publisher of the *New York Journal*, and Joseph Pulitzer, of the *New York World*.

Hearst and Pulitzer both envisioned a similar role for the press. According to this vision, newspapers would take an active part in exposing corruption, solving municipal crime, and amplifying the voices of those in need. Hearst summed up the spirit of this "journalism of action." He argued that "a newspaper, hardly less than a government, is the guardian of the people's rights."

These lofty ideas were challenged by changes occurring in the newspaper industry. Technological innovations had allowed papers to be printed in greater numbers and distributed over a wider area than had previously been possible. At the same time, papers were becoming more dependent on advertisers for revenue. This meant that having a high circulation was the determining factor in whether a newspaper would be successful or whether it would collapse. As a result, both Pulitzer and Hearst relied on lurid stories of scandal and murder to attract readers' attention. Competitive men, they also made significant improvements in newspaper design, layout, and specialization. These moves were all in an effort to undermine one another and sell more papers. Both the activist approach of the *Journal* and the *World* and their increasing reliance on sensationalized stories frustrated the other publishers in New York. Those papers took a more objective approach to the news. Critical of the way that Hearst and Pulitzer so often inserted themselves and their papers into the stories they printed, the resentful publishers embraced the term "yellow journalism." The phrase was a negative judgment of the style of reporting found in the *Journal* and the *World*.

The Looming Legacy of Yellow Journalism

Yellow journalism was characterized by media historian Frank Luther Mott as featuring prominent, attention-grabbing headlines, embellished or outright invented stories, and extreme sympathy for any perceived underdogs. Yellow journals also made wide use of illustrations, color comics, and, eventually, photographs. These qualities set the *Journal* and the *World* apart from their more respectable counterparts. Those newspapers maintained an even tone and a somewhat stricter dedication to the facts.

This difference was most clearly demonstrated in 1898, when the circulation battle between Hearst and Pulitzer reached its peak. The *World* and *Journal* both seized on an ongoing rebellion in the Spanish territory of Cuba as a source of outrageous stories. The two newspapers ultimately called for war after an American battleship exploded in Havana harbor. It would be wrong to say that the yellow journals were responsible for starting the ensuing Spanish-American War. Yet their hysterical coverage of the situation did convince readers of the necessity of war. This in turn made it easier for the American government, already looking for a pretext for war with Spain in the Caribbean, to launch an invasion with almost no public debate about its necessity.

Many of the technological and graphic innovations of the *Journal* and *World* continue to influence newspaper printing and design today. On the other hand, it is the misdeeds of the yellow press that now define the legacy of this period of journalism. The sensational style of reporting on world events, together with the overreliance on stories of scandal and crime, is a familiar problem to today's news consumers. News outlets' dependence on advertising revenue has only gotten worse since the days of Hearst and Pulitzer, influencing the tone and content of the news. Furthermore, the press's uncritical support of American foreign interventions in exchange for attention-grabbing stories has had terrible consequences throughout the twentieth and twenty-first centuries.

An independent, uncompromising press is a crucial part of any healthy democracy. The era of yellow journalism saw important steps taken toward the development of such a press. However, it also demonstrated the harmful tendencies this approach risks.

The Evolving Press

As the issues facing the United States changed during the late nineteenth century, so did the role of the newspaper. Over this period, the American press shifted from a largely partisan enterprise to a commercial one. In other words, newspapers went from acting largely as extensions of specific political parties to independent outlets. Once independent, newspapers became concerned with profit (and therefore advertising revenue) above all else. By 1865, the partisan press was an old institution. Partisan newspapers were now becoming a relic of the days when party insiders began publishing papers to dispense propaganda. Such papers were supported with funds from the party. Editors were

Founded in 1851, the *New York Times* was a relatively minor paper in the late nineteenth century, but it represented the kind of neutral, restrained reporting that Pulitzer and Hearst rebelled against.

hired to make the party and its candidates look good. If the editors succeeded, they would usually be rewarded with a better job in the administration of the winning candidate. If they failed, a new editor would be hired for the next election cycle.

By 1900, this type of press had largely been abandoned. Though there were still a handful of faithful party rags in the country, most papers had shifted to a more independent tone. Even papers that were ideological and tended to agree with either the Republicans or the Democrats no longer felt obligated to defend those parties at all times. These newspapers also covered more than just politics—entertainment, sports, comics, and, of course, colorful advertisements could all be found within their pages.

There were a number of reasons for this shift from a partisan to an independent, commercial press. For one, the expansion of the country and the simultaneous increase in its population led to a massive increase in the demand for newspapers. Along the East Coast, the American people were flocking to major cities as the country industrialized. At the same time, the arrival of vast numbers of European immigrants made these cities hotbeds of cultural and linguistic diversity. As a result, one or two local newspapers were no longer enough to satisfy the ever-growing populace.

Working-class Americans had different interests than upper- or middle-class Americans. New papers emerged to cater to these interests. Immigrant communities often started their own newspapers in the language of their home countries, for the benefit of those that had not learned to read English. Meanwhile, out west, newspapermen followed the early settlers along the frontier. As small towns were built around gold mines or oil wells, the communities that formed had need of a newspaper. The invention of the telegraph allowed journalists in these relatively isolated settlements to gather news from Chicago or New York. When combined with items of interest to the local community, this material was enough to produce a weekly edition of a newspaper (there usually were not enough reporters or editors to make a daily edition possible).

Many of these papers folded once the settlements were absorbed into larger towns and cities, but the demand for them demonstrated the growing desire of the American public for steady sources of news and other information. Over the course of the 1870s, the press expanded by 10 percent every year. In 1900, there were 2,200 daily papers and more than 11,000 weeklies in the country.

The increasing popularity of the penny press also changed the landscape of journalism. Invented in 1830, the penny press was exactly what its name implies—newspapers sold for a penny apiece. This affordable price allowed more Americans to read the paper on a regular basis. As a result, the kind of stories featured in the penny press began changing. Stories of crimes or tragedies befalling ordinary families proved to be a hit, as did tales of scandal. Many readers found this kind of reporting to be thrilling. By the late nineteenth century, penny presses were among the most popular papers in the country. They were, of course, in competition

The Civil War, Reconstruction, and the Changing Role of the Newspaper

A major factor in the shift of the newspaper from partisan tool to independent enterprise was the bloody Civil War (1861–1865) and its aftermath. The war had sparked an increased demand for straightforward reporting and objective *news*, rather than political commentary. Updates on the state of conditions on the war's front lines and reports of battlefield success or failure were prized over party propaganda. Different papers prioritized different elements of news gathering, including timeliness, exclusivity, accuracy, and sensationalism. Yet most outlets sought to provide readers with the on-the-ground reporting they were asking for. The assassination of Abraham Lincoln in 1865 reinforced the emerging role of the press, as editors rushed to be the first to report on the tragedy at Ford's Theatre.

The press also played an important role during Reconstruction, the twelve-year effort to reintegrate the Southern states into the Union and secure civil rights for the newly emancipated African American population. Southern newspapers fought against Reconstruction, standing by the Confederate cause and urging readers not to abide by the antiracism laws coming out of Washington, DC. While this crusade lined up very closely with the wishes of the era's Democratic Party, the Southern press was not motivated by pure party loyalty. It was instead motivated by a commitment to the issues of slavery and racial hierarchy. This type of issue advocacy would be echoed later in both Hearst's and Pulitzer's attacks on corporate and governmental wrongdoing.

The assassination of Abraham Lincoln by John Wilkes Booth was just one example of the increasing need for timely news reports in the second half of the nineteenth century.

with one another for readers and advertisers. Penny papers sought to be the first to report on certain stories and also began taking specific political positions on issues to differentiate themselves from their competitors. There was a limit to how far this editorializing could go, however. Since penny papers were sold so cheaply, they were dependent on advertising to keep them afloat. Therefore, papers had to be careful not to offend an advertiser and potentially lose a significant source of revenue.

The rise in advertising revenue (which made up 44 percent of the total revenue generated by publications in 1879 and 54.5 percent in 1899) also coincided with a fall in the price of paper stock. These circumstances allowed publishers to print more papers while also charging less for each copy. Papers got longer as well. Though newspapers had initially been between eight and twelve pages long, by the late 1870s publishers began adding in more specialized news (sports, entertainment, business, society,

This newsstand in Times Square shows the wide variety of newspapers available in New York City at the turn of the twentieth century.

etc.). These items first appeared in their own columns and eventually in their own sections. Both the lowered price of the paper and the expanded range of coverage enticed more people to purchase copies. The most successful papers were those that offered a wide variety of content.

By the end of the nineteenth century, the penny-press model of journalism had become dominant. The largest papers in the country were focused on reporting breaking news, as well as providing coverage of sports, fashion, gossip, and more. Sensationalized stories of crime and scandal were popular with readers. Editorials that took a clear stand on an issue of importance caused readers to either nod their heads in agreement or shake their fists in fury. Illustrations and political cartoons gave the papers a pleasing appearance, and advertisements filled out their pages and provided the vital financial support that allowed them to keep publishing.

Turn-of-the-Century Journalism in New York City

New York City, the United States' biggest metropolis and its financial backbone, was also the heart of the publishing industry in the late 1800s. The city boasted more papers than any other. Those papers set the agenda for the rest of the country. In the years before Hearst and Pulitzer arrived in New York, three papers dominated the city: the *New York Herald*, the *New-York Tribune*, and the *New York Sun*. The focus and direction of these papers was determined by their founders and editors. Each took a different approach to the news.

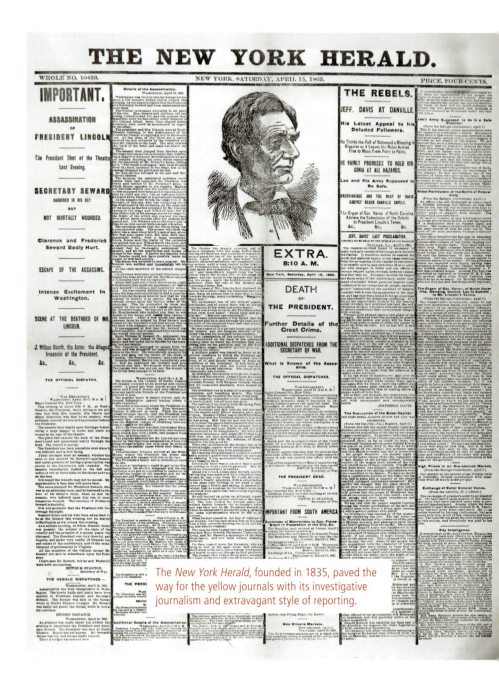

The *New York Herald*, founded in 1835, paved the way for the yellow journals with its investigative journalism and extravagant style of reporting.

James Gordon Bennett

The founder of the *New York Herald*, James G. Bennett, was a major figure in the world of newspaper publishing in New York and also an important influence on the yellow journalists who would follow in his footsteps. It would not be inaccurate to say that the attraction of his paper lay largely in its coverage of scandal and murder. Bennett focused on the seedier aspects of life in New York, reporting on subjects that were guaranteed to draw readers in. At the same time, Bennett was dedicated to quality journalism. He assigned reporters to cover the courts, police precincts, and New York high society, among other subjects. Bennett paid well for exclusive reporting and was always looking to break news. Though the *Herald* was at times loosely edited, its stories were for the most part accurate and detailed. The combination of dogged reporting and lurid subject matter served to make the *Herald* the most popular paper in New York during Bennett's time as its publisher. In his obituary for Bennett in 1872, rival publisher Horace Greeley wrote that Bennett "understood the value of news … He was the first journalist who went to meet the news half-way. That was the sole secret of his success."

As founder of the *New York Herald*, James Gordon Bennett sought to produce fact-based stories that also appealed to a mass audience.

The *New York Herald* was founded by James Gordon Bennett in 1835. Bennett dedicated the paper to pursuing interesting stories wherever they could be found. He wanted the stories in the *Herald* to stick to the facts. Bennett also believed in following up on his reporting and providing updates on ongoing stories until they concluded (or stopped being profitable, whichever came first). Bennett was succeeded in 1866 by his son, James Jr. Having been groomed for the position by his father, the younger Bennett found himself managing the paper mostly from Paris after a minor personal scandal. Under his long-distance leadership, the *Herald* continued to proactively seek out stories and look for exclusive scoops. In the most famous example of this intrepid reporting, the *Herald* in 1871 funded the expedition of Henry Morton Stanley into Africa, where he was tasked with finding the explorer Dr. David Livingstone. Stanley succeeded in his quest. The *Herald* triumphantly reported on the achievement, making sure to give itself credit for sponsoring the expedition in the process. Stanley was referred to in one article as "the chief of THE HERALD'S Corps of Search."

The *New-York Tribune* had been established in 1841 by Horace Greeley. Of the three major New York papers, it had the closest ties to the partisan press of the previous era. The paper matched the party lines of first the Whig and then the Republican Party, mirroring Greeley's own political views. Unlike his competitors at the *Herald* and the *Sun*, Greeley wanted the *Tribune* to feature a more objective style of reporting (an attitude shared by a smaller city paper, founded in 1851: the *New York Times*). Greeley became famous for his impassioned editorials, which were quoted by other papers throughout the nation. He also often allowed the targets of his criticism to respond with editorials of their own. By 1871, the weekly edition of the *Tribune* had a circulation of close to three hundred thousand.

The *New York Sun* was founded in 1833 as the first penny paper in New York. It was an almost immediate success. Selling eight thousand copies within its first six months (twice that of its nearest competitor), the *Sun* was cheaper than the other city papers. It also appealed to readers less concerned with political and business news. The paper was purchased by Charles A. Dana in 1868, who continued as publisher until his death in 1897. The *Sun* under Dana covered crime stories, popular lectures, and politics but also featured theatrical reviews and human-interest stories drawn seemingly from whatever Dana could see outside of his office window. Stories were run on everything from different styles of mustaches to strange flags he saw on ships in the harbor. Dana also paid for stories from several of the most well-known contemporary writers, including Robert Louis Stevenson, Walt Whitman, and Rudyard Kipling. These famous authors helped increase the prestige of the *Sun*.

By the early 1880s, the newspaper industry had undergone several dramatic changes. In New York City, the papers that had done the best job of adapting to these changes dominated the market. Over the course of the next fifteen years, however, two new papers would emerge as leaders in the field of journalism. They were helmed by two men of forceful personality, ceaseless work ethic, and unconquerable ambition.

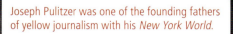
Joseph Pulitzer was one of the founding fathers of yellow journalism with his *New York World*.

The Storytellers

In many ways, the lives of Joseph Pulitzer and William Randolph Hearst were mirror images of one another. The future rivals both had strong personalities, high ideals, and a desire to change the world for the better. Each struggled to find his place before being given an opportunity to prove himself at small-market newspapers. Both turned those newspapers into industry juggernauts, revitalizing journalism in their communities. Each man then took what he had learned to New York City. In other important ways, the two men were vastly different. Pulitzer was born in eastern Europe, while Hearst was a child of the American West. Pulitzer, though not poor as a child, still struggled to make money during his first years in the United States. Hearst's father was a millionaire. Pulitzer also had greater scruples about the integrity of his newspaper than Hearst did. Though Pulitzer was just as enthusiastic

William Randolph Hearst got his start in the publishing industry in San Francisco and went on to found the *New York Journal*, the start of a national media empire.

a practitioner of "new journalism" as his future competitor, he felt a stronger attachment to the facts of the stories he reported than Hearst. This difference in outlook would ultimately come to a head when the two began warring with one another for readers in the 1890s. Long before that, however, both men were forming their philosophies of journalism and gaining experience in other parts of the country.

Joseph Pulitzer

Joseph Pulitzer was born József Politzer in Makó, Hungary, on April 10, 1847. His father, Philip, was a well-to-do Jewish grain broker. His mother, Louise, had brothers who were officers in the Austro-Hungarian army. His father retired shortly after Joseph's birth and moved the family to Budapest, where Joseph was educated in private schools and by tutors. Joseph was still a young boy when his father and eldest brother died, and he did not get along with his mother's new husband. Therefore, at age seventeen, Joseph left home, seeking to follow his uncles' lead and enlist in the army. Unfortunately for Joseph, his lanky, sickly build was not exactly army material. He was a tall man but very skinny, and his eyesight was extremely poor. In fact, he was effectively blind from 1890 until the end of his life and had to have most things (including people's faces) described to him visually. Young Joseph's gangly physique led to his rejection from several European armies.

Joseph Pulitzer was deemed unsuitable for military service, forcing him to search for a new profession in the United States.

From Hungary to the United States

Still desperate to join up, Joseph tried his luck with a Union army recruiter, who was in Germany looking for substitutes for American draftees into the Civil War. With the Union army in 1864 as desperate for men as Joseph was for a post, he was accepted into an all-German unit and arrived in Boston in September.

Joseph served in the army until the war's conclusion in April of 1865, at which time he went to New York looking for work. His search was unsuccessful. After dragging around the city for a while, he traveled to St. Louis, where there was a sizable German population and where he hoped his prospects would be better. Now an adult, Pulitzer worked a series of odd jobs by day and studied at the Mercantile Library by night, attempting to learn English and law. He also spent time in the library's chess room, where a group of wealthy German immigrants met on a regular basis. Through his connections in this room, Pulitzer was finally given his break. One of the men offered him a position as a reporter for a local German-language newspaper. Pulitzer seized on the opportunity and worked tirelessly at his new job. He outdid the rest of his colleagues and impressed his superiors with his creativity and work ethic. After a few years, he was offered a controlling interest in the paper by the owners, who were facing financial difficulties of their own. From there, Pulitzer was able to strike a series of shrewd business deals that ultimately allowed him to purchase the *St. Louis Post-Dispatch*, the most prestigious paper in the city, in 1878.

By this time, Pulitzer had become an American citizen and had mastered the English language. His position also made him a part of the St. Louis social elite, and he enjoyed attending fancy parties and going horseback riding. Having amassed a not insignificant fortune, he married Kate Worthington Davis, a Washington socialite.

Pulitzer had an endless intellectual curiosity and was constantly reading and doing things. At the same time, he maintained strong relationships with his wife and, later, his children. The writer Theodore Dreiser once described Pulitzer as "a man fighting an almost insane battle with life itself, trying to be omnipotent and what not else, and never to die."

From St. Louis to New York

Pulitzer threw himself into his work at the *Post-Dispatch* with relentless energy. He was at the paper's office from early in the morning until past midnight on a daily basis, supervising every aspect of its production. He wanted readers to understand that the paper was their champion. As a result, he did not hesitate to put investigative pieces and editorials attacking municipal corruption and rich tax dodgers on the front page. The integrity shown by this fearless journalism won him the support of the St. Louis public. The circulation of the paper boomed. The candor brought to the paper by Pulitzer did not play so well with the wealthy, however, who were unhappy with the *Post-Dispatch*'s exposure of the more sordid details of their lives. (These details included the often illegal shortcuts they employed to maintain their lavish lifestyles.)

By the early 1880s, Pulitzer was finding himself increasingly out of place in the circles he had formerly been a part of. Tensions boiled over in 1882 when Colonel Alonzo Slayback, a Democratic attorney, stormed into the office of the *Post-Dispatch*'s managing editor to complain about an insult he felt the paper had leveled at him. After some shouting, employees of the paper heard a gunshot. Rushing into the office, they found Slayback dead on the floor, a gun in his hand. The managing editor, John Cockerill, stood over him, insisting that he had shot Slayback in self-defense. Slayback's aide claimed that it was cold-blooded murder and that the gun had been planted on the colonel after his death. While a grand jury cleared Cockerill of all charges, upper-class St. Louis society believed the aide's side of the story. The scandal took its toll on Pulitzer, whose health was already declining as a result of the long hours he had been putting in at the paper. Together with his wife, Pulitzer prepared for an extended trip to Europe.

Planning to depart from New York, Pulitzer's plans changed when he arrived in the city and noticed that the *New York World*, a small publication with low circulation numbers, was for sale. The *World* had been founded in 1860 as a one-cent religious paper but had failed to find an audience. A number of changes in ownership followed, which saw the newspaper transformed first into a Democratic Party rag and then into a more nonpartisan newspaper. The *World* was later included in a bundle of stocks bought by the railroad baron Jay Gould in 1879 when he purchased the Texas and Pacific Railway Company. Under Gould's ownership, the paper again struggled to turn a profit. Gould, therefore, began looking for a buyer for the paper shortly before Pulitzer came to New York in 1883. Pulitzer jumped on the opportunity before him and started negotiating with Gould. Pulitzer ultimately purchased the *World* for $346,000, the amount Gould had paid four years earlier plus the losses he had suffered in the time since. It was a bargain for Pulitzer, who was able to enter the world of New York publishing at relatively low cost with a paper he was free to remake entirely. It also allowed him to escape the increasingly stifling world of St. Louis, where the publisher's confrontational style of journalism was beginning to have negative effects on his health.

Pulitzer brought his new brand of journalism to New York. He turned the *World* into an advocate for the common worker, both immigrant and native-born, and shone a spotlight on the corrupt practices of local businesses and government officials. He also included plenty of reports about street crime and lurid scandal, trusting the now well-established formula of attracting readers' attention.

The timing of Pulitzer's arrival in New York was incredibly fortunate for a man looking to make a name for himself and his publication. In 1884, the year after Pulitzer's acquisition of the *World*, Democrat Grover Cleveland ran for president against Republican James G. Blaine. While the other major New York papers

A physically imposing man, William Randolph Hearst was jovial with his employees but ruthless toward his competitors, determined to be the best at whatever he did.

Pulitzer
Sibling Rivalry

Albert Pulitzer, the younger brother of Joseph, had actually come to New York before his more famous sibling, and he was the first Pulitzer to get involved in the city's newspaper industry. Albert founded the *New York Morning Journal* in 1882, a year before Joseph purchased the *World*. The *Morning Journal* sold for a penny and published light gossip, entertainment news, sports coverage, and some bits of scandal. It rarely touched on politics and maintained an overall light-hearted tone. This proved to be a hit with workers and lower-class New Yorkers. The paper sold between 175,000 and 225,000 copies a year, putting it behind only the *Herald*, the *Tribune*, and the *Sun* in its circulation numbers. Those sales figures earned Albert a personal income of $100,000 a year.

Unfortunately for Albert, the good times were not to last. When Joseph arrived in New York and took over the *World*, one of his first acts as publisher was to hire away most of his brother's staff. This led to a break between Albert and Joseph, made worse as the *World* quickly surpassed the *Morning Journal* in popularity and revenue. Tensions simmered over the next decade as the *World*

Sharp Fighting Begins Along the River Drina on the Bosnian Frontier.

COUNTER INVASION PLAN

May Strike First at France.

Berlin dispatches state that Ger-many has made it quite clear to St. Petersburg that even "a partial mo-bilization" will be answered imme-diately by the mobilization of the Ger-man Army, which, according to one dispatch, "nothing could then hold back."

"Minister of Foreign Affairs of Austria."

Russia Announces Its Wish to Remain at Yet Is Determined to Guard Its

Albert Pulitzer, Joseph's younger brother, was also part of the New York publishing scene in the late nineteenth century. He did not have his brother's success, however, and Albert's most enduring legacy is his founding of what would eventually become Hearst's *New York Journal*.

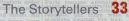

Albert Pulitzer sold the *Morning Journal* in 1895.

became more and more successful. Albert finally snapped in 1894. For reasons known only to himself, Albert decided to *raise* the price of the *Morning Journal* to two cents a copy in order to directly compete with his brother. This move failed spectacularly. Half of the *Morning Journal*'s circulation vanished almost overnight with the higher price. Stubbornly pursuing his quest for vengeance for several more months, Albert finally admitted defeat in 1895 and sold the *Morning Journal* to an interested buyer. Albert used the money from the sale to travel to Europe, where he resided until he took his own life in 1909.

threw their support behind Blaine, the *World* endorsed Cleveland. New York's Democrats flocked to Pulitzer's paper in response, swelling its circulation numbers. At the same time, disputes between James Bennett, news dealers, and advertisers over the price of the *Herald* and the cost of advertising within its pages allowed Pulitzer to sweep in and undercut his competitor in both areas.

Pulitzer sold the *World* for less (two cents a copy against the *Herald*'s three-cent asking price) and also sold advertising space at a cheaper rate than the other major papers. Within a year, Pulitzer was able to turn around the fortunes of the *New York World*. He was poised to become one of the most important publishers in the city.

William Randolph Hearst

The man who eventually posed the biggest challenge to Pulitzer's domination of the New York City publishing industry was William Randolph Hearst. Of the two rivals, Hearst is the more well-known, and he has gone down in history as an almost mythical figure. Part of the reason for this is that Hearst's career lasted far longer than Pulitzer's. Hearst was still an influential publisher and politician well into the middle of the twentieth century. But his reputation is also partly due to the influence of Hearst himself. Both in his own writings and in his choice of biographers, Hearst attempted to craft the legend of his own life. He successfully created a romantic origin story that glossed over his many contradictions. He was born into immense wealth but insisted that nothing had been handed to him. He began his career battling

George Hearst

William Randolph's father, George Hearst, was born in 1820 or 1821 (the exact date is uncertain) in Missouri. Poorly educated, Hearst went into mining as a young man. After many years of unsuccessful digs, he finally struck it rich in 1859 with a silver mine in present-day Utah. Returning home to Missouri to care for his ailing mother and to find a wife, Hearst courted Phoebe Apperson, a schoolteacher more than twenty years his junior. Though the two were opposites in almost every way (Phoebe was intelligent and refined, George uneducated and vulgar), they married in 1862. Phoebe gave birth to her only son a year later.

Hearst's investments made him a millionaire. He used the money to purchase further mining claims, as well as real estate holdings. This led to periods of high profit but also times of significant losses when the stock market contracted and the prices of gold, silver, and copper dropped. The Panic of 1873 in particular put a squeeze on Hearst's finances. It took several years for his various mining ventures to make up for his losses. During this time, Hearst spent most of the year away from home, overseeing his various investments. This put a strain on his marriage. Phoebe wished that her husband would spend more time with her and William, while George

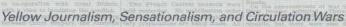

George Hearst made a fortune in mining and other investments before being elected to the United States Senate as a Democrat near the end of his life.

felt more at home in the environment of a mining camp. Phoebe occasionally made brief visits to George on the road, and George would occasionally be home for a few weeks at a time. However, neither partner was happy in the world of the other. George nevertheless managed to maintain an amicable relationship with his son, and George ultimately gave William his start in the newspaper business.

occasionally have to sell some of their furniture, and, at one point, their house, gave William a lifelong fear of financial instability.

Young William was a healthy child but not athletic or rugged. He often acted out as a boy. Later in life, William reflected that this might have been his way of attempting to be seen as a man by his father. Like Joseph Pulitzer, William obtained his education through a series of private schools and tutors. His schooling, however, was constantly interrupted. Phoebe Hearst regularly pulled William out of classes to accompany her on visits to her family or to go on trips abroad, including one eighteen-month-long voyage to Europe. Despite the financial burdens occasionally faced by the family, George never stopped extending his wife a line of credit for her expenses. George attempted to ensure that Phoebe and William were affected as little as possible by his changing fortunes.

Rejuvenating the *Examiner*

In his early adulthood, William Randolph Hearst found himself directionless after being expelled from Harvard for a prank. Searching for a place to direct his ambitions, he asked his father if he could try his hand at running the *San Francisco Examiner*, a newspaper George had come to own in one of his many financial transactions. Though the elder Hearst thought his son would hate the job, William insisted. Therefore, in 1887, George Hearst legally transferred ownership of the unprofitable paper to his son. George also promised to

NS

Vil-

the
ion,
wing
r in-
ome
ary,"
that
tele-
con-
that
sen-
iery-

One,
as
con-
il-
the
tion
mal
and
rm
the
ity
not
or
ons.

em-
ion
ut-
the
s-
u-
th-
the
er-
ide
of
ints
re.
ed
u-
to-
ont
b-
on
ly,
ur
va-
ce
v-
en
or
ve
d
i-
ion
ned
and
an,
in
r

PRINTERS TO EXPOSE ANTI-HEARST PLOT

ST. PAUL, June 18—The Board of Governors of the Allied Printing Trades Association met again to-day to consider further action in condemning what was said to be a bitter political plot against William Randolph Hearst and his newspapers.

It was decided to send the resolutions denouncing the conspiracy adopted Monday to the 25,000 local unions of all trades in the country, every city central body and State Federation of Labor.

Matthew Woll, the president, said the members of the Board of Governors wanted the trades unions of the country to know the facts and thereby expose the political crusade.

WILSON TOLD BY GOMPERS OF TENDER

Labor Chief in Telegram Warns President Strikes Will Follow Action of Western Union Tel.

By INTERNATIONAL NEWS SERVICE

ST. PAUL (Minn.), June 18.—President Wilson, in which he declined to accept the latter's recommendations, created a furore to-day in the American Federation of Labor convention.

S. J. Konenkamp, for the telegraphers, and J. P. Noonan, for the electricians, declared a strike of both trades was certain, if the Western Union "insisted upon organizing its employees into a union, to be controlled by the company."

After President Gompers had read Carlton's reply he sent this telegram to President Wilson, pointing out the danger of a strike:

The convention of the American Federation of Labor unanimously instructed me to convey to you the protest of the delegates constituting the convention against the action of Newcomb Carlton, of the Western Union Telegraph Company, in issuing a call for a convention of employees of the Western Union, for the purpose of perfecting an industrial constitution, in order to control all employees, the expenses of the convention to be paid by the company.

The action of the company is intended as a continuation of its policy of denying its employees their right to belong to a bona-fide, legitimate trade union, and refusal to reinstate employees discharged because of membership in a trade union affiliated with the American

INDIAN FRESCO UNCOVERED AT OLD MISSION

Freize, Hidden in Dolores Sacristy Perhaps for More Than a Century, Brought to Light

Brought to light after having been hidden for more than a generation, a fresco of supposed Indian handicraft was unearthed yesterday on one of the crumbling adobe walls of the old Mission Dolores.

The fresco, which is in bright carmine, ochre and blue-gray, was found by Policeman Charles E. Fennell, who lives in Mission Dolores parish and has taken a lifelong interest in the historic chapel, where he was christened.

SCROLL REVEALED.

Fennell, watching workmen engaged in buttressing the walls of the building, had his attention attracted by streaks of color flashing from peeling kalsomine on what was once the interior of the old sacristy. Mounting a ladder, Fennell dug into the kalsomine with a pocketknife and soon had exposed part of what looked like a scroll or similar geometrical design.

He kept prying under the white layers, which fell off in large blotches, and presently had uncovered a space about four feet long and two feet wide.

The general scope of the design could be followed, and although the details were obscured, it appeared to be Indian or Spanish-Indian in treatment. One of the details looked like a horseshoe, and what resembled a hand on a running or gesticulating figure of a man could also be discerned.

The fresco could be followed as a frieze running between decorative bands along the top of the wall. It was painted with pigments that appear to have retained much of their original brilliance. The place where it was found was the interior of the south wall of the old sacristy.

Originally this sacristy, extended out as an L-wing from the chapel proper, and it was later abandoned for a sacristy built behind the carved gilt altar.

Fennell, who has taken an active part in the restoration of Mission Dolores, called the attention of Father John Sullivan to the fresco.

HIDDEN FOR YEARS.

"Neither Father Sullivan nor any one else in the parish heard of this fresco before," said Fennell. "The old sacristy walls were preserved with a sheathing of wood by Father Pendergast away back in 1862, but the kalsomine I peeled off to-day was undoubtedly on the walls then, and the probability is that the presence of the fresco was unknown at that time. Mission Dolores was built 142 years ago, and it may be that this fresco dates back to 1776. Some of the professors of the Affiliated Colleges who have specialized in Indian lore may be able to express an opinion as to that. The fresco should certainly be an interesting thing for them."

The small sum of—

$5.00

Births, Engagements, M

BORN.

ARCHBOLD—In this city, June 13, to the wife of J. A. Archbold, a son.

ANDERSON—In this city, June 17, to the wife of F. E. Anderson, a son.

BALL—In this city, June 18, to the wife of W. H. Ball, son.

BROCK—In this city, June 13, to the wife of S. Bruno, a daughter.

BAILEY—In this city, June 13, to the wife of D. B. Bailey, a daughter.

BERNARD—In this city, June 13, to the wife of H. F. Bernard, a daughter.

CHRISTEN—In this city, June 14, to the wife of W. Christen, a son.

CONLAN—In this city, June 11, to the wife of S. L. Conlan, a son.

De BARR—In this city, June 11, to the wife of J. M. De Barr, a daughter.

ESCUDO—In this city, June 11, to the wife of A. A. Escudo, a son.

FLAHERTY—In this city, June 13, to the wife of J. J. Flaherty, a daughter.

FIELDS—In this city, June 10, to the wife of R. J. Fields, a daughter.

GALLAGHER—In this city, June 14, to the wife of E. M. Gallagher, a son.

HENDRICK—In this city, June 14, to the wife of J. G. Hendrick, a daughter.

HANDWRITH—In this city, June 14, to the wife of M. L. Handwrith, a son.

KERR—In this city, June 3, to the wife of J. L. Kerr, a daughter.

KAUFMAN—In this city, June 14, to the wife of A. O. Kaufman, a son.

KING—In this city, June 13, to the wife of H. King, a daughter.

KNUDSEN—In this city, June 13, to the wife of A. K. Knudsen, a daughter.

LONG—In this city, June 11, to the wife of K. Long, a daughter.

LUGAR—In this city, June 2, to the wife of N. Lugar, a son.

MILLER—In this city, June 13, to the wife of C. T. Miller, a daughter.

MILLER—In this city, June 11, to the wife of H. Miller, a son.

MAHONEY—In this city, June 14, to the wife of D. Mahoney, a daughter.

OLSON—In this city, June 13, to the wife of B. Olson, a son.

O'CONNELL—In this city, May 31, to the wife of Dennis O'Connell, a son.

PADKER—In this city, June 14, to the wife of L. Padker, a daughter.

PLUMMER—In this city, June 11, to the wife of P. R. Plummer, a daughter.

SHEA—In this city, June 13, to the wife of John Shea (nee Murray), a son.

SCHWARTS—In this city, June 13, to the wife of E. Schwarts, a son.

STRICKER—In this city, June 14, to the wife of E. Stricker, a daughter.

SAUNDERS—In this city, June 14, to the wife of E. Saunders, a son.

SCHAEFER—In this city, June 17, to the wife of E. Schaefer, a daughter.

SULLIVAN—In this city, June 16, to the wife of P. Sullivan, a daughter.

TRUMPOM—In this city, June 18, to the wife of J. G. Trumpom, a daughter.

MARRIAGE LICENSES.

The following marriage licenses were issued up this city yesterday:

ALVARADO—DE SENNA—Anthony L. Alvarado, 43, 586 Second avenue, and Mina J. De Serna, 23, 513 Van Ness avenue.

BOYER—MURPHY—Theodore K. Boyer, 21, Oakland, and Alice L. Murphy, 19, 967 Eighteenth street.

JEMAYEMA—FAY—William S. Berryen, 31, Oakland, and Augusta C. Fay, 18, 458 Noe street.

CRAVEN—TILLINCH—Alexander R. Craven, 21, Ft. Scott, and Jenny Tillinch, 29, Merrill, Wis.

DICK—JENSEN—Mitchell C. Dick, 30, and Emma B. Jensen, 24, both of Stockton, Cal.

DURAN—CABAREZ—Hipolito Duran, 42, 1239 Stockton street, and Apolonia Cazarez, 23, 1632 Mason street.

FONG—WONG—24 C. Fong, 29, 831 Market street, and Constance Wong, 26, 809 Sacramento street.

FITZPATRICK—GRINDOFF—James D. Fitzpatrick, 35, Los Angeles, and Ethel R. Grindoff, 21, Elizabethton, Conn.

GRANT—HASTINGS—Martin H. Grant, 24, 441 Noe street, and Julia Hastings, 48, 649 Noe street.

IIJIMA—IKEDA—Nisuo Iijima, 41, 738 Stockton street, and Shime Ikeda, 24, 2413 Webster street.

LEVY—LEARY—Morris H. Levy, 31, 1969½ Dupont street, and Adele G. Karsky, 18, 1299 Fell street.

LAURENCE—GABRIEL—Joseph F. Laurence, 31, 5161 Holetete street, and Ozeolia G. Gabriel, 31, 2471 Bryant street.

PERRALL—TRACY—Francis J. A. O'Ferrall, 25, Santa Clara, and Ann K. Tracy, 24, 517 Florida street.

PERRY—HARRIS—Roy M. Perry, 26, Fort Baker, and Jewell Harris, 22, Berkeley.

PIGEN—SKELLOV—James A. Pierce, 33, 1467 Sacramento street, and Jessie A. Skellow, 22, Chicago.

STORKE—BORDINET—Robert E. Storck, 27, 918 Fourteenth street, and Estelle H. Bordinet, 24, 588 Howard street.

Louise Ritter, grandmother of Ella Ritter and Maria, Clara and Ruth, wife of Germany, aged 69 years, 7 days.

Friends are invited to attend services to-morrow (Thursday) at 9 a. m., at her late residence, 385 —, — (Funeral arrangements under the — F. Bohr & Co.)

BAYLESS—In this city, June 17, 1918, beloved husband of Olga Bayless, Eugene, George and Leonard Bayless, England, aged 43 years. Friends are invited to attend the funeral (Wednesday), June 19, 1918, 2 m., at Truman's chapel, 1919 near Fifteenth. Interment, Cypress —.

BIFFORD—In this city, June 18, beloved wife of the late Samuel F. and mother of Mrs. Frances V. Oakes and Charles M. Bifford, a native of —, aged 72 years 10 months and — days. Friends and acquaintances are —

CANFA—In this city, June 14, Canepa, dearly beloved husband of Mrs. M. Carmelia, a native of Italy, 58 years 1 month 11 days. Friends and acquaintances are —

CLEMENT—In this city, June 14, 7, loved son of Edmond and —, late loving brother of Valentine, Willie Clement, a native of San Francisco of the Milmen's Union No. 42. Friends and acquaintances are invited to attend the funeral Wednesday, June 19, at 8:45 a. m., from the late residence, 24 Hartford street.

COONEY—In this city, June 16, 1917, loved wife of Daniel J. Cooney and mother of James F. Anderson, a native of —, aged 64 years.

EDWARDS—In this city, June 17, T., beloved husband of Bridget —, of London, England. A member Lodge, Sons of St. George. Friends and acquaintances are invited to attend the funeral Wednesday, 1918, at 9:30 a. m., from late Norfolk street; thence to St. Joseph —.

FAYER—In this city, June 17, Francis C. Favier, beloved husband Father Favier and father of Frances Jess Favier, a native of Baltimore. Funeral private.

FOSTER—In Oakland, June 17, beloved wife of William W. Foster of Berkeley, Cal.

GRIFFI—In this city, June 28, and a native of Italy, aged 54 years. Services to-morrow (Thursday) at the chapel of Mahned & Co., 1? Interment, Italian Cemetery.

GRANT—In this city, June 18, beloved son of Alfred N. Grant, band of Mary A. Grant, beloved and Mrs. Mand I. Thomas of Florence A. and Elizabeth —, brother of Mrs. William Hartnett of Maine, age 43 years, of Yerba Buena Lodge No. —, and State of Maine Society. Friends are invited to attend the funeral Wednesday, June 29, from —; thence to St. Joseph's, Ashby & McMullen, 2255 Sixth street, Geary and Clement —.

GREEN—In Alameda, June 18, 1919, beloved husband of Amanda Green, father of Joseph S. Green and Badley, a native of Ireland, and months 11 days. Friends and are respectfully invited to attend the Funeral and Interment Thursday, at France.

HALLORAN—In San Rafael, June 17, cheal B., beloved husband of Mary and devoted father of Marie Ann Halloran and brother of Mrs. — and Belle H. Halloran, a native of —, aged 65 years, a member of the Lodge No. 26, I. O. O. F. Friends are invited to attend services Thursday, June 20th, from of F. E. Keeyer, 708 Fourth street —; thence to St. Raphael's Church requiem mass will be said for the — of the soul, commencing at 9 o'clock a. m. Mt. Olivet Cemetery. Remains at the F. E. Keeyer, 1002 Fourth street, —

HARROVER—at rest, in this city, June Jane Roberts Harrover, dearly beloved William Harrover and loving mother Basil Harrover and loving sister Lizie and John C. Roberts and daughter-in-law John S. and Marion I. Roberts, California. Blue Lodge members are invited to attend the funeral Thursday, 1918, at 2 o'clock p. m., from the Golden Gate Undertaking Co., 7 street, near 31st, Interment, the —

An issue of the *San Francisco Examiner* from 1918, after Hearst's time as publisher, nevertheless vows to expose an "anti-Hearst plot."

relaxed. After his first few years as publisher, Hearst's editorial oversight began to slacken. Exaggerations or outright fabrications started entering the paper, written by reporters either desperate to please the boss or, in some cases, too lazy or incompetent to file a proper story. In one such incident, Hearst instructed Eddie Morphy, one of his reporters, to profile seven notable San Franciscans for the Sunday edition of the paper. After coming up with six people to feature, Morphy found himself stuck and proceeded to invent a seventh profile to meet his quota. His creation, an orphan boy raising his two younger brothers, attracted the most attention. Sympathy for the poor boy's case prompted an outpouring of donations to the paper, including $100 from Hearst's own mother. Tasked with getting the money to his fictional source, Morphy panicked and eventually decided to find some random children on the street, dress them in rags and take their picture, and then use the money to buy them new clothes. A rival paper, the News Letter, later revealed Morphy's deception. Though some employees resigned in protest at the misrepresentations and falsehoods being used to drive circulation, the paper continued to be successful. Hearst began looking to expand into a larger market.

Coming to New York

When George Hearst died in 1891, his fortune was split between his wife and son. Though Phoebe Hearst hoped that William would now spend more time in high society, make a nice marriage, and settle into the idleness of wealth, he was too much his father's son. Hearst disdained the pretensions of aristocratic society and wanted to purchase another newspaper. Spending time at the offices of the *Examiner*'s East Coast bureau in New York, he began looking for a paper in the city in the fall of 1895.

Of the forty-eight daily papers serving the 1.5 million residents of New York at the time, Hearst was most attracted to the *Morning Journal*, the small, struggling publication that had been founded by Albert Pulitzer, Joseph Pulitzer's younger brother. Pulitzer had sold the paper only a few months earlier, and its new owner had been unable to halt its slide. Drawing on his own inheritance and using his mother's fortune as security, Hearst purchased the paper for $150,000. Simplifying its name to the *New York Journal*, Hearst immediately brought in a group of his best reporters and editors from San Francisco.

Looking at the New York media landscape, Hearst realized that his stiffest competition would be the *New York World*. It was the only other major paper in the city using a similar style of aggressive journalism. Over the previous decade, Joseph Pulitzer had made it the most popular daily in New York. Determined not to be outdone, Hearst began copying some elements of the *World*'s style in the *Journal*, and he dropped the price of the *Journal* to a penny per copy. He was supportive of the Democratic Party and aimed his stories at the same working-class audience that had been responsible for the success of the *World*. With the *Journal* providing the same type of reporting at half the cost, Pulitzer's readers began drifting to Hearst's paper. The rivalry that would come to define the next four years was born.

THE EVENING JOURNAL'S **CIRCULATION** IS GREATER THAN THE COMBINED CIRCULATION OF **ALL THE OTHER** NEW YORK EVENING NEWSPAPERS

THE 20TH CENTURY NEWSPAPER.

NEW YORK JOURNAL

EVENING EDITION

W. R. HEARST.

QUEEN EXTRA

NO. 6,641—P. M.　TUESDAY.　NEW YORK, JANUARY 22, 1901.　Copyright, 1901, by W. R. Hearst.　TUESDAY.　PRICE ONE CENT.

QUEEN VICTORIA DEAD

Aged Monarch Passed Out of Life Without a Struggle as if Going Asleep.

Special Cable to the Evening Journal.

London, Jan. 22.—Queen Victoria, Empress of India, is dead.

She passed from life without a struggle. Her end was painless. She expired as one sinks into sleep.

At her bedside when death came were many whom she loved, among them were the Prince of Wales, now King Edward VII, who will be known as King and Emperor; the Princess of Wales and their son, the Duke of York; Princess Louise, Princess Battenberg, Princess Beatrice, the Duke of Connaught, the German Kaiser and Prince Christian. With them were her physicians, Sir James Reid, A. Douglass Powell, her surgeon, Sir Francis Henry Laking, ladies of her court, her devoted friends and some of her oldest attendants.

Among these were her faithful servant from India who helped the Queen in her daily walks about her rooms and who always stood behind her chair while she was dining.

So expired, with all that loving care could do to soften the dread ordeal, the most conspicuous character of the Victorian age, the most distinguished British sovereign since William of Orange.

As the readers of the Evening Journal know, her death was not unexpected. For some time it was known that the vital powers of the Queen were slowly failing and, while the shock is great only the great sorrow of the people will mark the end of the longest reign in English history.

All had been prepared for the political change, and the accession of Albert Edward to the throne will cause no disturbance in business or State affairs.

But the people mourn. No queen, not even Elizabeth, was loved by Britons as Victoria has been loved ever since she took the sceptre a simple girl. The evidences of grief are seen and heard in every city and hamlet in the mourning emblems and the tolling bells.

It is a world sorrow which the death of the aged monarch has brought; for her rule belted the earth, and in far-distant countries and in every clime Englishmen and sons of Britons will mourn her. And in many foreign lands her children and their children rule and the mourning of the European courts, so inevitable and usually so perfunctory when sovereigns die will have in it personal grief.

It is yet too early to say what will be the funeral ceremonies. That she will be given a burial suitable to her supreme station among rulers is undoubted, of Englishmen in their great queen will demand. express commands, if she left such with those in whom she placed her confidence, will prevent it.

Her body will be buried by the side of her husband consort—him whom she mourned so deeply, for whom she maintained almost an austerity of grief during all the years of her long widowhood.

The tomb of the Prince is at Frogmore, on the Isle of Wight, almost within sight of Osborne House, where the Queen died. It was this fact which made Osborne the favorite residence of the Queen.

The accession of the Prince of Wales will probably be without further ceremony than the usual proclamation, the notification of foreign Governments, and the surrender of the seals by the important Ministers of the Crown for reappointment.

HER MAJESTY, QUEEN VICTORIA.

A typical issue of the *New York Journal* from 1901 not only brags about the size of the paper's circulation but also uses a screaming banner headline (with the word "DEAD" made extremely prominent) to report on the elderly Queen Victoria's entirely natural passing.

The Yellow Journals in Action

"There was never before anywhere on Earth such a rivalry, and, God willing, there never will be again," remarked Charles A. Dana, publisher of the *New York Sun*, about the competition between William Randolph Hearst and Joseph Pulitzer in New York City. Pulitzer had taken the city by storm in the 1880s, bringing a new style of journalism to the metropolis and transforming his *New York World* from a forgotten rag into the most popular paper in the city. When Hearst arrived on the scene in 1895 and his *New York Journal* began directly competing with Pulitzer, a circulation war was inevitable.

Hearst and Pulitzer were vying with one another for the attention of the New York City reading public and the advertising revenue that would come with the higher circulation number. The rivalry led to a number of impressive innovations in publishing, as well as some high-quality journalism. It also led to a relaxation of editorial standards and a desperate need for more and more outrageous material. The ensuing product appalled the other publishers in New York, who used the epithet "yellow journalism" to describe the papers being published by Hearst and Pulitzer.

A Closer Look at Yellow Journalism

The negative connotation attached to the term "yellow journalism" is well-deserved. The *Journal*, the *World*, and smaller papers that followed in their footsteps committed serious misdeeds. The tendency of these papers to exaggerate or outright invent stories is unforgivable, and the fact that their publishers were often unwilling to issue corrections for obvious errors is shameful. Sensationalism, though it had always existed to some extent, was taken to new extremes by Hearst and Pulitzer. While both tried to stick to their populist, voice-of-the-people roots and train their editorial fire on the failings of big business and government, even those stories fell victim to embellishment as competition intensified.

At the same time, much of what modern readers take for granted in print newspapers was established by the yellow journalists. Headlines stretching across the entire width of the front page and the idea that the front page of the paper could contain a variety of different topics (including illustrations) were innovations of the late nineteenth century. The extensive use of graphics and cartoons by the yellow journals has survived into modern times, as has the reliance on anonymous sources to assemble sensitive stories. Pulitzer and Hearst wanted their papers to cater to as wide an audience as possible. Therefore, they reported on local, national, and world news, sending correspondents around the country and across the globe. In 1898, the *Journal* estimated that it spent around $15 million covering the Spanish-American War. Pulitzer and Hearst also invested in presses that printed in multiple colors, allowing them to publish colorful Sunday supplements. Finally, production runs were timed to coincide with train schedules to make it as convenient as possible for readers to get freshly delivered copies of the paper. These practices were adopted by papers throughout the country in the late nineteenth and early twentieth centuries and have continued to influence the field of journalism through to the present day.

The *World* Takes Over

Upon his arrival in New York in 1883, Joseph Pulitzer surveyed the state of the city's largest papers. The *New York Herald* ran from eight to twelve pages and was sold for three cents, while Charles Dana's *New York Sun* charged two cents for a sparse four pages. Dana intended for the *Sun* to be read all the way through rather than browsed, hence its small size. The *New-York Tribune*, following the death of Horace Greeley in 1872, had drifted in a conservative direction. It was by then a solidly Republican paper, selling for four cents. Other

Telegraph offices were a boon to the growing newspaper industry in the late nineteenth century, as they allowed reporters and editors to communicate over vast distances in a relatively short amount of time.

Technology and
the New Journalism

The technological changes taking place in the late nineteenth
century played a major role in the development and spread
of the style of journalism practiced by Joseph Pulitzer and
William Randolph Hearst. Electrically operated machinery,
industrialized presses, and new systems of typesetting
combined to increase newspapers' production capacity,
allowing them to print more copies in a shorter period of time.
In 1887, forty-eight thousand copies of an eight-page paper
could be produced in an hour. By 1892, that number had
doubled. Thanks to increased production capacity, publishers
had the freedom to extend deadlines and begin printing
evening editions of the paper.

Other technologies helped in the gathering of news and
the distribution of finished papers. The telegraph allowed
reporters in the suburbs to transmit news back to their
office in the city center and also enabled editors to wire
instructions to their reporters while on assignment. The
invention of the telephone made this process even faster. The
automobile, starting in the early twentieth century, allowed
both reporters and newspapers to travel faster and farther than

or make more money. This problem was much worse at the *Journal*. There, as had happened at the *San Francisco Examiner*, stories were padded or outright fabricated, often by exhausted, broke employees.

The Rise of the *Journal*

Hearst's arrival in New York in 1895 provided another jolt to the city's publishing world. The established papers were still reeling from the phenomenal success of Pulitzer's *World* when another, younger publisher (Hearst) came onto the scene and began publishing a paper that was even more uncompromising and sensational than the *World*. Pulitzer himself was also shocked. He had operated the most successful paper in the city for many years and had not yet experienced competition this serious in his time in New York. The *Journal* began eating away at the *World*'s circulation numbers almost immediately after Hearst assumed control. Then Hearst dropped the price to a penny, undercutting Pulitzer's two-cent daily.

Hearst was able to corner an opening in the market in much the same way that Pulitzer had more than a decade earlier. Pulitzer had used the presidential election of 1884 to position his paper as the voice of the Democratic New York working class. Hearst did the same in 1896, when the Democrats ran William Jennings Bryan against Republican candidate William McKinley. Bryan, running on a platform of economic populism, was looked at skeptically by even Pulitzer. Pulitzer felt the Democratic nominee's proposals went too far. Though the *World* did not dismiss Bryan entirely, there

Three-time Democratic nominee for president William Jennings Bryan ran a populist campaign in 1896 that was supported by the *New York Journal*.

keep pace with his rival led to the *World* growing more sensational by the day, the other publishers in New York reacted with horror. Though their papers had reported on crimes and scandal, the over-the-top nature of the coverage in the *Journal* and the *World* was seen as excessive. Moreover, the activist journalism practiced by Hearst and the strong editorial stances taken by Pulitzer were perceived as running counter to the spirit of journalism. Journalists, it was understood, should stick to the facts and report them objectively.

Some publishers were also uncomfortable with the fact that the *World* and the *Journal* had a mostly working-class audience. They did not like that newspapers were no longer the preserve of the upper class. As a result, led by Charles Dana and Ervin Wardman, the publisher of the *New York Press*, the established papers of New York called for a boycott of the *Journal* and the *World* in the winter of 1897. The boycott encouraged libraries, social clubs, YMCAs, and other institutions to stop carrying copies of the offensive "yellow journals." Though nearly one hundred institutions in New York and New Jersey did ban the papers, the boycott ultimately failed. The *Journal* and the *World* were far and away the most popular papers in the city, with circulation numbers in the high six figures. A moral crusade by their competitors was doomed to fail. The yellow journals were undeniably more entertaining and possessed more energy than any other paper in New York. No one was going to stop reading them in favor of their more boring counterparts. Ironically, the boycott may have actually *increased* sales of both the *Journal* and the *World*, as people that would have otherwise read the papers at their club or library instead had to buy their own copies.

The failure of the boycott proved that, for the time being at least, the yellow journals reigned supreme in New York City. Hearst, confident in his position, embraced the yellow journalism epithet in 1898. He boasted that "the sun in heaven is yellow—the sun which is to this earth what the *Journal* is to American journalism." With the other papers neutralized for the time being, the rivalry between the *Journal* and the *World* only intensified. Each publisher viewed the other as his only real competition. Pulitzer had come to acknowledge Hearst's skill at attracting attention to his paper and began questioning whether his hesitation to go all in on sensationalism and embellishment was holding him back. A crisis in the Caribbean would resolve this matter in Pulitzer's mind. The subsequent behavior of the *World* and the *Journal* would plainly demonstrate the very real dangers of yellow journalism.

Why "Yellow Journalism"?

Political cartoons were an important part of the appeal of both Pulitzer's *World* and Hearst's *Journal*. They helped the publishers in their efforts to expose corruption and hypocrisy in business and in government and also attracted new readers to the papers. They proved especially crucial during the lead-up to the Spanish-American War. Political cartoons are also tied into the rivalry between the two publications, however, and a cartoon is responsible for inspiring the term "yellow journalism."

On one of the many fronts of the war between Hearst and Pulitzer was the cartoonist Richard Outcault. He was the artist behind *Hogan's Alley*, the most popular comic in New York. Published in the *New York World*, the comic depicted a group of tenement-dwelling children who regularly mocked upper-class customs. Their ringleader was known as the Yellow Kid due to the color of his clothing. The Yellow Kid was irreverent, hyperactive, and very popular with the New York reading public. Hearst successfully lured Outcault from the *World* to the *Journal* in October of 1896 and began publishing Yellow Kid cartoons in the pages of his own paper. Furious, Pulitzer let another cartoonist draw a set of rival cartoons, also featuring a child in yellow clothing.

It was this incident that stuck in the mind of Ervin Wardman when he began calling for a boycott of the *World* and the *Journal* in 1897. Searching for a clever phrase to describe the papers, he eventually settled on "yellow-kid journalism." Wardman effectively used the subject of the papers' most petty feud to symbolize their larger lack of standards or integrity. The term was soon shortened to "yellow journalism" and became the go-to descriptor for Hearst's and Pulitzer's methods of publishing.

The Yellow Kid of the *New York World* was the inspiration for the term "yellow journalism."

The explosion of the USS *Maine* in Havana harbor resulted in a circulation war in New York City and an actual war in the Caribbean.

The Yellow Press Sells a War

The circulation battle that raged between Joseph Pulitzer's *New York World* and William Randolph Hearst's *New York Journal* peaked in 1898. That year, the rival publishers abandoned what little claim to objectivity they still possessed in their coverage of the Spanish occupation of Cuba. Stories of Spanish atrocities brought to New York by Cuban refugees were woven together to form a narrative depicting peaceful, freedom-loving Cubans being crushed under the iron boot of Spain. These sensational stories were used by the *Journal* and the *World* to drive their circulation numbers ever higher. Pulitzer even reversed his previous dedication to accuracy in the stories he published.

After the USS *Maine* exploded in Havana harbor under mysterious circumstances, the yellow papers immediately blamed the Spanish. Again, it would be going too far to say that yellow journalism caused the Spanish-American War. But when the American government declared war against Spain in April, the *Journal* and the *World* were staunchly supportive. The over-the-top coverage in the most popular New York dailies certainly convinced the American people to support the war. More important, it allowed the government's motives for going to war—which were decidedly *not* purely humanitarian—to go unquestioned and unchallenged.

The yellow press essentially served the function of a propaganda department, establishing a dangerous precedent in the relationship between the press and American foreign policy that continues to the present day.

The Cuban Rebellion and the Yellow Press

The crisis in Cuba began in 1895, when twenty-five thousand to thirty thousand rebels rose in revolt against Spanish rule. The island of Cuba was one of Spain's last colonial possessions and was crucial to the country's economy. The Cuban people did not benefit from being colonial subjects, however. They were saddled with high taxes and commercial regulations designed to help the domestic economies of both Spain and the United States. Spain's forceful methods of maintaining control over the island, including the suppression of a previous revolt, also contributed to the 1895 rebellion. The rebels, ordinary citizens drawn from all walks of life, fought a guerrilla war against the Spanish. Rebels burned down sugar plantations and attacked military outposts. Their goal was to damage the island's infrastructure and economy to such an extent that Spain would grant the territory independence out of sheer frustration. In other words, the rebels hoped to make the cost of hanging onto Cuba higher than the revenues it brought into the Spanish treasury. If that plan failed, the rebels hoped that the US military would intervene to secure American economic interests, which were also threatened by the instability.

Spain responded to the rebellion with excessive force, dispatching two hundred thousand soldiers to Cuba in an effort to defeat the rebels. The soldiers were led by General Valeriano Weyler y Nicolau. His insistence that "war should be answered with war" prompted Hearst to refer to him as "the Butcher" in the pages of the *Journal*. Of the many brutal tactics used by Weyler to crush the revolt, none was worse than his policy of "reconcentration." In order to deprive the rebels of food and logistical support, rural Cubans were herded into fortified towns and cities against their will. These reconcentration camps were lacking in food and sanitation. Starvation and disease were rampant. Cuban civilians began dying in waves as a result. In one town, twenty-five to thirty-five people died per day and were buried in mass graves. Of the four hundred thousand Cubans taken to reconcentration camps, between ninety-five thousand and two hundred thousand died.

A cigar card depicts a heroic charge by Cuban rebels during the Cuban revolt.

COMBATE DE "ALTAGRACIA"

The brutality of the Spanish made its way to New York through Cuban refugees and sympathizers, whose stories were taken at face value by Pulitzer's *World* and Hearst's *Journal*. Beginning shortly after the rebellion broke out in 1895, both papers began turning to Cuba as a reliable source of material. The events happening there were shocking and violent—and of constant interest to the reading public. According to a 1934 study by Joseph Wilson, between 1895 and 1898 fewer than twenty days went by without a story about Cuba in the major New York newspapers. The stories in the *World* and the *Journal* were written in a sensational manner, painting the Spanish as black-hearted villains bent on destroying the defenseless Cubans. "The horrors of a barbarous struggle for the extermination of the native population are witnessed in all parts of the country," proclaimed the *World*. "Blood on the roadsides, blood on the fields, blood on the doorsteps, blood, blood, blood!"

Political cartoons were also weaponized in the crusade against the Spanish, who were depicted as vultures or other menacing figures looming over Cuban women and children. Other cartoons went after President William McKinley for his hesitation to enter a war against Spain. One memorable image depicts McKinley holding back Uncle Sam, who is preparing to charge with a drawn sword toward the Spanish eagle as it descends on a helpless Cuban woman. "Let go of him, McKinley!" reads the caption.

There was no shortage of stories coming out of the island, especially once a censorship program launched by Weyler led to the arrest of a *World* reporter, prompting a yearlong campaign in the paper to secure his release. In their quest to outdo one another, however, Hearst and Pulitzer made obvious errors and also committed acts of questionable legality. On one occasion, the *Journal* reported with outrage that a woman had been strip-searched by Spanish officers aboard a ship departing Cuba. In reality, the woman had been privately searched by female customs officers, in full compliance with standard procedure. These kinds of mistakes only ever went in one direction—toward demonizing Spain. The most notorious stunt pulled by the *Journal* during this time involved a young Cuban woman named Evangelina Cisneros. The eighteen-year-old daughter of one of the rebels, Cisneros had been arrested in July of 1896. Cisneros's arrest came after she allegedly attempted to seduce a Spanish official. She insisted that the officer in question had in reality broken into her home and attempted to assault her before her screams attracted some friends, who helped rescue her. Despite the witnesses who backed up Cisneros's version of events, she was imprisoned without a trial.

When the case came to the attention of Hearst, he reacted in characteristically bombastic fashion. Declaring Cisneros "a pure flower of maidenhood" who was "guilty of no crime save that of having in her veins the best blood in Cuba," he launched a signature-collecting campaign to demand the release of "the Cuban girl martyr." Though the campaign was supported by many prominent Americans, including several important women (among them Clara Barton, Julia Ward Howe, President McKinley's mother, and the widow of former president Ulysses S. Grant), it failed to secure Cisneros's freedom. Undeterred, Hearst sent Karl Decker, one of his reporters, to Cuba with instructions to get Cisneros out of jail and bring her back to New York. With the help of some local accomplices, Decker succeeded in breaking Cisneros out of prison and smuggling her back to the city. Though Hearst's journalism of activism had now clearly crossed the line into flagrant illegality, the *Journal* nevertheless celebrated the rescue as "epochal" and "the greatest journalistic coup of this age." Decker was praised for his "superb audacity and dashing intrepidity." Six issues of the paper were devoted to the affair in October 1897. The American people celebrated the *Journal*'s accomplishment. Various quotes praising the paper were printed under the headline "AMERICA'S WOMEN AND STATESMEN APPLAUD THE *JOURNAL*'S FEAT."

Headed Toward War

At the same time that the American public began turning against Spain, relations between the American and Spanish governments worsened. In February of 1898, Cuban rebels managed to get their hands on a private letter written by the Spanish ambassador to the United States, Enrique Dupuy de Lôme. In the letter, addressed to a colleague, de Lôme criticized President

MAINE EXPLOSION CAUSED BY BOMB OR TORPEDO?

Capt. Sigsbee and Consul-General Lee Are in Doubt---The World Has Sent a Special Tug, With Submarine Divers, to Havana to Find Out---Lee Asks for an Immediate Court of Inquiry---Capt. Sigsbee's Suspicions.

CAPT. SIGSBEE, IN A SUPPRESSED DESPATCH TO THE STATE DEPARTMENT, SAYS THE ACCIDENT WAS MADE POSSIBLE BY AN ENEMY.

Dr. E. C. Pendleton, Just Arrived from Havana, Says He Overheard Talk There of a Plot to Blow Up the Ship---Capt Zalinski, the Dynamite Expert, and Other Experts Report to The World that the Wreck Was Not Accidental---Washington Officials Ready for Vigorous Action if Spanish Responsibility Can Be Shown---Divers to Be Sent Down to Make Careful Examinations.

The New York World a day after

The front page of the *New York World* the day after the explosion of the *Maine* was already speculating that a bomb or a torpedo was responsible for the damage.

McKinley. De Lôme even called him a "low politician" who was "weak and catering to the rabble." Sensing the impact this letter could have, the rebels smuggled the letter to the *Journal*. Hearst did not hesitate to print the letter in its entirety on February 9, describing it in an irresponsibly hyperbolic headline as "THE WORST INSULT TO THE UNITED STATES IN ITS HISTORY." The outrage caused by the publication of the letter was widespread. It prompted both de Lôme's resignation and a formal Spanish apology. The scandal was short-lived, however, as further events in Cuba wiped the letter from the front pages less than a week later.

The USS *Maine*, an American battleship, had been sent to Cuba in early 1898 after a series of riots had taken place in Havana, sparked by Spanish residents frustrated at the prospect of an independent Cuba. The *Maine* was officially docked in Havana harbor as part of a friendly visit to the island. However, its true purpose was to protect American citizens and business interests in the city and to transport American citizens to safety if the situation worsened. The ship was manned by a crew of 329 enlisted men and 26 officers. At 9:40 p.m. on the night of February 15, while the city of Havana celebrated carnival, crew members on the *Maine* heard a small explosion on the port side of the ship, near the bow. An instant later, a second explosion tore through the vessel, lifting it out of the water and raining down bits of wood, steel, and flesh over a radius of 0.5 miles (0.8 kilometers). The massive fireball was seen by everyone in the harbor. Lifeboats were immediately launched to search for survivors in the wreckage. Of the 355 men aboard the ship at the time of the explosion, 266 were killed instantly or succumbed to their wounds. Among the survivors, only 16 had managed to escape the flames without injury.

Occurring when it did, at a time of rising tensions between Spain and the United States and less than a week after the publication of the de Lôme letter, the sinking of the *Maine* was perceived throughout the United States as a deliberate act of sabotage by the Spanish government. Both Hearst and Pulitzer ran with this version of events without waiting for any facts to come in, as it provided a perfect climax to the narrative of the sinister Spanish they had been building for the better part of three years. "DESTRUCTION OF THE WAR SHIP *MAINE* WAS THE WORK OF AN ENEMY," proclaimed the *Journal* on February 17. The subhead stated, "NAVAL OFFICERS THINK THE *MAINE* WAS DESTROYED BY A SPANISH MINE." On the same day, the *World* asked, "*MAINE* EXPLOSION CAUSED BY BOMB OR TORPEDO?" In the pages of both papers, and in the minds of their readers, Spain's guilt was predetermined. War was presented as the only possible response. Both the American and Spanish governments launched inquiries into the sinking of the *Maine* and presented two different explanations for the disaster. The Spanish determined that an accidental explosion inside the hold of the ship had ignited the powder magazine. The American inquiry concluded that the initial explosion had occurred outside of the ship, meaning the *Maine* had been mined either intentionally or through sheer negligence. In either case, the inquiry said, Spain was to blame. It was no surprise that the yellow journals, and the American public, chose to believe this version of events. In 1976, a retired US Navy admiral finally presented overwhelming evidence that a fire inside one of the *Maine*'s coal bunkers had been the source of the explosion, proving the Spanish verdict of an accidental explosion correct. Unfortunately, this resolution came nearly eighty years too late.

President McKinley submitted a war resolution to Congress on April 11, 1898. Within ten days the United States and Spain were formally at war. The Spanish-American War lasted for less than four months, from April 25 to August 12, 1898. It was exhaustively covered by the *Journal* and the *World*. Both papers spent millions of dollars on correspondents and other methods of newsgathering. During the height of the war, Hearst and Pulitzer each boasted a circulation of over 1.6 million daily papers. Coverage of the war was decidedly nationalist in tone, recounting the heroic deeds of the American soldiers and insisting on the superiority of American values. In fact, the conflict's reputation as a "splendid little war" was in large part due to its presentation in the press as a wholesome adventure, carried out for clear moral reasons with no lasting consequences.

This was just as much of a fiction as any of the *Journal*'s or the *World*'s sensationalized articles. The war was not as simple as it was presented in the

William McKinley, president from 1897 to 1901, oversaw the Spanish-American War and the acquisition of foreign colonies that resulted from it.

newspapers, which had failed in their stated purpose of being critical of the government's actions and policies at a time when skepticism was most warranted. This is not to say that yellow journalism caused the Spanish-American War. In fact, the anecdote often cited as proof that William Randolph Hearst instigated the war is a myth. (That myth involves a telegram he supposedly sent to his photographer with the instructions, "You furnish the pictures, and I'll furnish the war.") The yellow press did help sell the war to the American people, however, laying out a humanitarian argument that could be used by the government as a pretext for a war it had been longing to fight for other reasons.

The Spanish-American War

The United States in the late nineteenth century was a nation looking outward. Influenced by the closing of the western frontier and new theories about the importance of a powerful navy in the development of nations, American politicians began focusing on expanding the country's influence overseas. The European powers had established colonies in Africa and Southeast Asia, prompting American imperialists to look for ways to exert influence in the Caribbean, Central America, and the Pacific. Fueled by the same spirit of manifest destiny that had led to the expansion of the United States across the entirety of the continent, expansionist politicians like Theodore Roosevelt and Henry Cabot Lodge wanted to spread American values beyond the nation's borders. They hoped to earn the country a degree of international prestige in the process. Other expansionists saw imperialism as an economic necessity. With a growing population and increasingly productive industrial capacity, the country needed markets in which to sell its surplus goods. The depression of the early 1890s and a series of strikes by organized labor throughout the 1880s and 1890s only seemed to strengthen the case of the economic imperialists. Hawaii, where the American government had supported the overthrow of the native monarchy in 1893, and Latin America were the primary markets seen as essential to continued economic prosperity in the United States. This played a major role in the start of the Spanish-American War.

By the late 1890s, the United States had $50 million invested in Cuba and was doing more than $100 million worth of trade with the island. Moreover, American exports of steel and oil were worth nearly $1 billion in 1898, and many of the trade routes used by American ships went through the Caribbean. The revolt in Cuba, and the instability brought to the entire region as a result of the increase in Spanish ships, disrupted this trade. In short, it hurt American business interests. In McKinley's instructions to the American ambassador to Spain, the economic impact of the rebellion was highlighted as the primary reason the United States wanted to see an end to the hostilities. No mention was made of the plight of the ordinary Cuban civilians. The United States also neglected to send any kind of aid to the rebels or even officially recognize their struggle,

Seen here in the uniform he wore to lead the "Rough Riders" into combat in Cuba, Theodore Roosevelt was one of the staunchest expansionists in the government in the late 1890s and was eager to see a war with Spain.

suggesting that the Cuban cause was of no real concern to the American government. Instead, imperialists in the government had been drawing up plans since at least 1896 for how to go about fighting a war with Spain in the Caribbean. By 1897, Theodore Roosevelt, the assistant secretary of the navy, was outlining the opportunities and pitfalls presented by a war in his letters. In November, he wrote, "I believe that war will have to, or at least ought to, come sooner or later." Roosevelt believed in war as an exercise in masculine virtue and had been agitating for a military response to the Cuban situation for years before the war officially began. Though he privately admitted that there was no way to prove that Spain had been responsible for the sinking of the *Maine*, he enthusiastically supported the war anyway. He even resigned from the Navy Department in order to personally lead a unit of soldiers into combat.

The Spanish-American War was therefore the end result of an American government growing increasingly concerned with economic expansion and imperialism and preparing for the inevitability of a military confrontation with Spain. The *Maine*'s explosion was little more than a pretext, a convenient way of insisting that the United States had been *forced* into the conflict and had no selfish motivations. Looked at in this context, the yellow press served the function of a marketing department for the war effort. Motivated by greed and ego, Hearst and Pulitzer competed to see who could present the most outrageous story about

Spanish brutality, all the while making it easier for the government to justify a war that might have otherwise seemed opportunistic and unnecessary. The chief of the Bureau of Foreign Commerce, an official in the larger Commerce Department, reflected years later that the war was part of a "general movement of expansion." He stated that the war was seen as necessary to "find foreign purchasers for [American] goods" and to make "access to foreign markets easy, economical, and safe."

The treaty that formally ended the war also reflected the self-interest underlying the United States' involvement in the conflict. Cuba was granted its independence, but the new government was forced to include an amendment in its constitution granting the United States the ability to forcibly intervene in the country's affairs at the discretion of the American government. The United States also inherited several new colonies from the Spanish, including Puerto Rico, Guam, and the Philippines. These territories gave the United States a position of dominance on the world stage. They also gave the country a number of new markets in which American goods could be sold. When a group of Filipino rebels rose up against American rule in 1899, the United States, which had only a year earlier claimed great sympathy for oppressed revolutionaries, launched a brutal three-year campaign to suppress the revolt. More than seven thousand American soldiers were killed or wounded in the fighting. And more than two hundred thousand Filipinos lost their lives as well, a scale of devastation that far surpassed that of

Pulitzer's Prizes

Following the Spanish-American War, Joseph Pulitzer backed away from the worst excesses of yellow journalism in an effort to salvage his reputation. Refocusing the *World* on the exposés of corruption that had made it popular in the first place, he broke major news in 1909 when his paper reported on a fraudulent $40 million payment made by the American government to the French Panama Canal Company. President Theodore Roosevelt was livid that the paper had published this information and attempted to bring a libel charge against Pulitzer, but the courts threw it out. The story was Pulitzer's last major scoop.

Having previously criticized the wealthy for dying with millions of dollars gathering dust in their bank vaults, Pulitzer was determined to do something good with his money before his death. His ultimate dream was to establish a school to train the next generation of young journalists. He realized his ambition when he donated $2 million to found the Columbia University School of Journalism. He also established a series of prizes as inducements to excellence. Bearing his name, the Pulitzer Prizes would recognize outstanding achievement in

In addition to establishing the Pulitzer Prizes, Joseph Pulitzer founded the Columbia School of Journalism.

not only reporting and editorial writing, but also in literature, history, music, and biography. The Pulitzer Prizes are still awarded on an annual basis.

Joseph Pulitzer died aboard his yacht in 1911. In his will, he expressly forbade his heirs from selling the *World*. Though the paper had managed to improve its reputation in the last decade, its popularity steadily waned as time went on. By 1930, the paper was losing $2 million a year. In 1931, it was sold to, and merged with, the *Evening Telegram*.

Pub⁴ & for Sale by J L Magee 34 Mott S⁴ NY

GEN: LOPEZ THE CUBAN PATRIOT GETTING HIS CASH

LOPEZ. Well; we have not Revolutionized Cuba, but then we have Got what we came for, my Comrades came for
Glory, I came for Cash, I've Got the Cash, they've Got the Glory, & I suppose we're all satisfied.
I'm O_P_H. for the United States again. Can't Live under a Millitary Despotism

Even after the conflict ended, Americans' feelings
about the Spanish-American War ran high, as
evidenced by this 1899 political cartoon.

the conflict in Cuba. The war fought in the Philippines was not glorified or even extensively reported on in the American press, yellow or otherwise. Atrocities committed in the name of imperialism were only good copy when they were committed by other governments, apparently.

The Legacy of Yellow Journalism

The end of the war also represented the end of the rivalry between Hearst and Pulitzer. Though both the *Journal* and the *World* continued to publish for the next several decades, their owners' attitudes toward the papers changed after the peace. Pulitzer emerged from the fog of war ashamed of his lowered standards. He had abandoned his principles in order to pursue money and circulation numbers. His professional reputation had suffered as a result. By the early 1900s, he had determined to return to his roots, campaigning against governmental and business corruption. Hearst, meanwhile, now had his sights set on running for political office. The *Journal* continued to "make" the news. Hearst, however, stepped away from day-to-day operations in 1899 to focus on political campaigning for himself and other candidates he supported. With its two main practitioners focused on other things, the era of yellow journalism came to a sudden and surprising end. More sober papers, like the *New York Times*, became popular in the early decades of the twentieth century. Yet the legacy of the yellow journals remained visible in even the most strait-laced of their replacements.

Hearst After Cuba

William Randolph Hearst's career extended deep into the twentieth century and involved the creation of a media empire as well as several political campaigns. After turning over daily control of the *Journal* to an associate in 1899, Hearst mounted a successful run for the House of Representatives in 1902. He additionally launched failed runs for the presidency, governorship of New York, and mayoralty of New York City in the decade that followed. Despite these losses, Hearst never stopped promoting his own image.

By the early 1910s, he had built an empire of eight newspapers and two magazines, and he had become one of the most famous men in the country. Twenty years later, his newspaper audience numbered twenty million people. He was also invested in radio, film, and newsreels. In his later years, Hearst drifted steadily to the political right. He fought against Franklin Roosevelt's New Deal policies and was a staunch anticommunist. In fact, the Hearst of the 1940s would likely have denounced his younger self as a dangerous radical. As he got older, he also increasingly eccentric. He used

Yellow Journalism, Sensationalism, and Circulation Wars

William Randolph Hearst speaks during his campaign for mayor of New York City in 1909. Hearst launched several bids for office in the 1900s, most of which failed.

sensationalism A journalistic technique in which events are reported in a hyperbolic, or exaggerated, manner, usually designed to present the story with a particular slant and evoke a specific emotional response. This can lead to inaccurate reporting or to stories being assigned greater importance than they actually possess.

weekly A newspaper printed once a week.

yellow journalism Popular in the late nineteenth century, a style of reporting that relied on exaggerated or invented stories of scandal and crime to attract readers' attention. Yellow journalism also featured attacks on powerful interests from the common man's perspective, heavy use of political cartoons and other illustrations, and a belief that newspapers should actively make the news, not simply report it in an objective fashion.

Further Information

Books

Campbell, W. Joseph. *Yellow Journalism: Puncturing the Myths, Defining the Legacies*. Westport, CT: Praeger, 2001.

Morris, James McGrath. *Pulitzer: A Life in Politics, Print, and Power*. New York: HarperCollins, 2010.

Nasaw, David. *The Chief: The Life of William Randolph Hearst*. Boston: Houghton Mifflin, 2000.

Websites

New York Journal Collection, Library of Congress

https://www.loc.gov/collections/new-york-journal

Issues of the *New York Journal* from 1896 to 1899 are archived here, allowing viewers to read the yellow journal for themselves and to experience its sensational headlines and stories firsthand.

The Pulitzer Prizes

http://www.pulitzer.org

The website for the Pulitzer Prizes includes a biography of Joseph Pulitzer, information about the prizes' history and selection process, and a complete list of previous winners.

Yellow Journalism, PBS

https://www.pbs.org/crucible/frames/_journalism.html

As part of the companion website for the documentary *Crucible of Empire*, the section on yellow journalism includes background information on William Randolph Hearst and his reporter Richard Harding Davis, as well as galleries of headlines and political cartoons related to the Spanish-American War.

The Yellow Kid on the Paper Stage

http://xroads.virginia.edu/~MA04/wood/ykid/yj.htm

This website focuses on the Yellow Kid, the cartoon character that inspired the term "yellow journalism," detailing his origins, the social criticism contained in his comics, and how he eventually faded into obscurity.

Films

Citizen Kane (1941)
Available on Blu-Ray and DVD

Orson Welles's 1941 masterpiece tells the story of Charles Foster Kane, a newspaper publisher, politician, and media magnate. The character was based on William Randolph Hearst.

Crucible of Empire: The Spanish-American War (1999)

This PBS documentary details the events leading up to the Spanish-American War, the course of the fighting, and the consequences in both the United States and around the world; commentary by historians and excerpts of primary sources add depth to the presentation.

Spencer, David R. *The Yellow Journalism: The Press and America's Emergence as a World Power*. Evanston, IL: Northwestern University Press, 2007.

Topping, Seymour. "Biography of Joseph Pulitzer." The Pulitzer Prizes. Retrieved September 20, 2017. http://www.pulitzer.org/page/biography-joseph-pulitzer.

Whyte, Kenneth. *The Uncrowned King: The Sensational Rise of William Randolph Hearst*. Toronto, ON, Canada: Random House Canada, 2008.

Zinn, Howard. *A People's History of the United States*. New York: HarperCollins Publishers, 2005.

Index

Page numbers in **boldface** are illustrations.

About the Author

Brett Griffin earned a degree in history from Canisius College, with a focus on American and European history. Other Cavendish titles written by Griffin include *The Interwar Years: Weimar Germany and the Rise of Fascism* and *History Makers: Sitting Bull, Native American Leader*. In addition to history, Griffin is also passionate about film, music, and literature, and he enjoys pursuing those interests in his spare time. He lives in Buffalo, New York.